Pathfinder 15

A CILT series for language teachers

Improve your image

The effective use of the OHP

Daniel Tierney
&
Fay Humphreys

C*i*LT

Other titles in the PATHFINDER series:

Reading for pleasure in a foreign language (Ann Swarbrick)
Communication re-activated: teaching pupils with learning difficulties
 (Bernardette Holmes)
Yes - but will they behave? Managing the interactive classroom
 (Susan Halliwell)
On target - teaching in the target language (Susan Halliwell and Barry Jones)
Bridging the gap: GCSE to 'A' level (John Thorogood and Lid King)
Making the case for languages (Alan Moys and Richard Townsend)
Languages home and away (Alison Taylor)
Being creative (Barry Jones)
Departmental planning and schemes of work (Clive Hurren)
Progressing through the Attainment Targets (Ian Lane)
Continuous assessment and recording (John Thorogood)
Fair enough? Equal opportunities and modern languages (Vee Harris)

First published 1992
Copyright © 1992 Centre for Information on Language Teaching and Research
ISBN 1 874016 04 6

Cover by Logos Design & Advertising
Printed in Great Britain by Oakdale Printing Co Ltd

Published by Centre for Information on Language Teaching and Research, Regent's College, Inner Circle, Regent's Park, London NW1 4NS.

All rights reserved. No part of the publication may be reproduced, stored in a retrieval system, or transmitted in any form or by any means, electronic, mechanical, photocopying, recording, or otherwise, without the prior permission of the Copyright owner.

Contents

		Page
1.	Making the case for the OHP	1
2.	Presenting new language	4
3.	Language games	9
4.	Supporting the target language	14
5.	Teaching grammar	16
6.	Songs and stories and surveys and things	18
7.	Siting and using the OHP in the classroom	20
8.	The 'raw materials'	22
9.	Technical know-how	26
10.	In conclusion ...	37
Appendix: Maintenance and care		38

Acknowledgements

We would like to thank

- ★ our colleague, John Henderson, of the AV & Media Education Section of Jordanhill College for his valuable support and imaginative genius in producing some of the examples we have used here, for his advice throughout, in particular for the appendix on maintenance and care of the OHP.

- ★ Laura Jardine, P.G.C.E. student, Jordanhill College 1991-92 for the sunglasses acetate (figs 6 & 7).

- ★ Patricia Dobson, National Development Officer, SOED for the idea for fig 11.

1   Making the case for the OHP

Modern linguists use an extensive range of resources - flashcards, cassette recorders, perimeter labs, computers, video and in some cases, even satellite television and interactive video. All serve to enhance the quality of the language programme. Amongst all this plethora of 'state of the art' technology there is, available for most teachers, the **overhead projector** - one of the simplest and yet most versatile resources which the language teacher possesses and one which is frequently undervalued and used in the most sterile of ways, as a substitute blackboard, as a device for projecting screeds of notes for transcription, even as a lectern! While we would agree that some of these are valid and convenient uses of the equipment, they only exploit a tiny fraction of its total use to the language, or indeed any other, teacher.

The OHP has so much more to offer the language teacher. Used in an imaginative and versatile way, it can prove an invaluable tool in support of good classroom practice.

- ★ It can enhance and expand group and pair work;
- ★ it stimulates use of the target language by pupils;
- ★ it can ensure progression by building up situations from the simple to the complex;
- ★ it enables the teacher to use the target language for instructions and convey meaning effectively through easily manipulated visual clues, both for spoken and written language;
- ★ step by step teaching using overlays helps to clarify difficult concepts;
- ★ revising and reinforcing vocabulary and structures can be made more lively and interesting;
- ★ it is a useful tool in practising, developing and extending language skills.

The ease of use and the flexibility of the OHP gives it advantages over some other standard classroom tools.

> ★ The work surface is horizontal and of manageable size;
>
> ★ teacher and class are face to face all the time (highly desirable, particularly in some classes!);
>
> ★ projection is satisfactory with normal daylight - no need for blackout;
>
> ★ teacher can work comfortably, free from chalk dust;
>
> ★ it is easy to refer back to previous points (not possible if you've wiped the chalkboard clean);
>
> ★ it can be used as an enlarging tool;
>
> ★ it can provide a backdrop for shadow theatre work;
>
> ★ used in conjunction with a tape recorder, it can become an exciting story telling device.

OHP transparencies are easy to produce, versatile and durable.

> ★ They are time saving - once prepared, they can be used, filed and re-used many times;
>
> ★ they are more versatile and dependable than flashcards;
>
> ★ for the non-artistic they offer the ease of tracing;
>
> ★ they allow for movement to be included;
>
> ★ they can be a powerful motivator, particularly for young learners.

In this book we hope to

★ suggest to you some innovative uses of the medium;

★ help in the production of high quality software;

★ indicate the basic procedures of care and maintenance.

Chapters 2 - 6 deal with methodology and show how the OHP can be used effectively for language input, language games, real communication, model exercises, support for the target language, grammar, posters, songs, story telling, and to organise group work.

Chapters 7 - 9 deal with the practicalities of preparation of good quality transparencies and of the most efficient use of the OHP in the classroom.

O.K., we can hear you saying: 'That's all the wrong way round. You should have the 'how to do it sections first!' We realise this, but the first part of the book is the carrot. By the time you've read it we hope that you'll be desperate to get into the practicalities and develop your own ideas as well as implementing ours.

Incidentally, we are not advocating that the OHP should dominate your teaching. Everyone is an individual with his or her own style of presentation, but we hope that we can convince you that there is a great potential for development here and that your imagination will be stimulated to an even more exciting and creative extent.

2   Presenting new language

New language can be presented in a variety of ways. One of the most effective of these is using the OHP.

Alternatives to flashcards

Flashcards have many plus points and we are not advocating discarding them. However, six to eight illustrations can sit comfortably on one transparency - all clearly visible and **all** facing the same way! Is there a language teacher in the country who has not at some time or other presented a sideways cinema or an upside down footballer to a mocking class? Transparencies can be put, and kept, in gender order. The illustrations are visible to you as well as the class without the undignified gyrations or loss of eye contact with the class.

Fig 1

Bringing in the written form is simple - flick over an overlay and then, by flicking over a further overlay, introduce the written form of the language.

Silhouettes

Any solid object with a clearly defined shape - e.g. a pen, a pencil or a key will show up in silhouette. Cut stencils and bought shapes will produce the same effect!

Telling the time

Toy clocks with movable hands have presented us with problems - the hands indicating a different time from what we expected. These problems are most elegantly overcome when the OHP is used. Indeed commercial masters (e.g. Mary Glasgow's *Timesaver* series - appendix 1) are on the market and both analogue and digital clock faces can be obtained. However, it is worth inserting a small word of caution at this point. Photocopying on to acetate is the last stage **after you have planned ways in which the material is going to be presented to the class** (fig. 2).

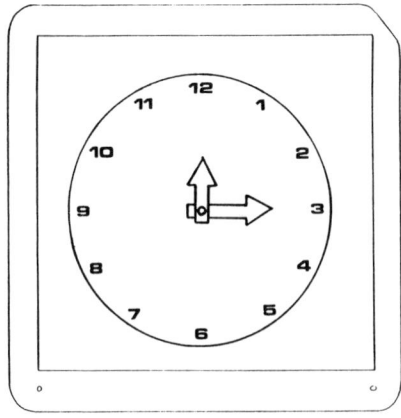

Brass paper fastener through the cardboard cut out hands and the acetate has its 'prongs' folded back and is taped down with masking tape on the back of the acetate.

Fig 2

Young children enjoy manipulating the hands as a part of language recognition or in setting the question for the class. The written form, both question and response, can be brought over as overlays on the analogue version thus assisting children to grasp the concept. But always think your use of the transparency all the way through before instigating the headlong rush to the photocopier.

A slightly more sophisticated OHPT allows you to link time with talking about daily routines, travel, school subjects, even television programmes and many other possibilities (figs. 3 and 4).

Analogue clock assembled as in fig. 2.

Fig 3

5

Fig 4   A hole is cut in each acetate so that it will fit directly over fig. 3 to allow manipulation of the clock hands.

These transparencies could be re-used as different tenses were encountered, and could be totally non language specific, bringing in the written language by means of an overlay if desired.

The weather

A different and fun way of presenting weather phrases can be provided if weather symbols are combined with maps of the UK or the country of the target language. Pupils can recognise the new phrase, choose the appropriate symbol and position it on the correct place. Using maps of local areas pupils can experience the 'pleasure' of placing symbols where they choose, e. g. 'rain' in the neighbouring district and 'sun' in their own, if they say the correct phrase. This would obviously not be a good idea if inter-district rivalry in the class was at an unhealthy level!

Directions

Straight ahead, turn left, turn right can easily be shown on a simple OHP diagram. An overlay can extend this to indicate first, second and third. Using a silhouette or a cut out transparency of a car or bicycle, we can add the fun element. A further overlay with town places can be added as cut out shapes (fig. 5).

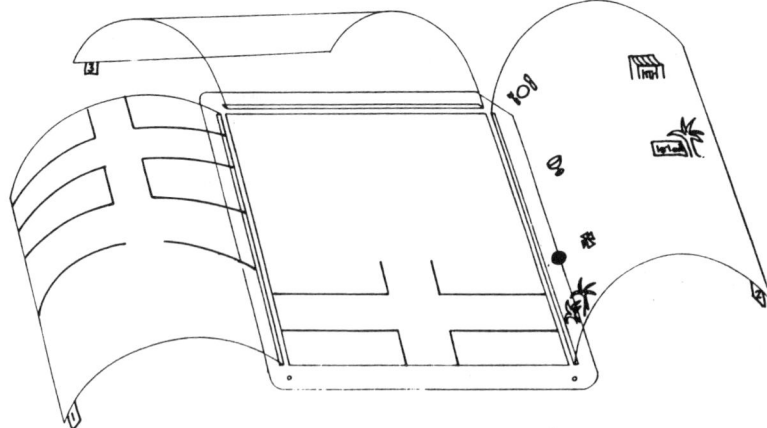

The blank overlay (3) is always useful so that you can write on the unit and remove it later, leaving the basic information untouched.

Fig 5

Descriptions

Personal descriptions can be built up by starting with a face outline and adding, on overlays, short/long hair with different colours. This can be extended to include eyes, etc. You can become more adventurous and add silhouette shapes like fun sun glasses - all adding to the amount of language which can be developed (figs. 6 and 7).

1. short dark hair
2. long fair hair
3. short brown hair
3+4 long brown hair

Obviously, other combinations are possible.

Fig 6

Fig 7   Series of 'fun' sunglasses shapes, cut out in card.

Clothes

Clothes can be added to models on an OHP transparency. If possible, children working in pairs should each be given a set so that they can all carry out the activity at the same time. Young pupils in particular enjoy this activity and the language of clothes can be combined with the language of colour. But remember, the overlays are transparent so be prepared to see the body outline under their clothes!

Furniture and room layouts

Furniture in a room can be arranged using either acetate or silhouette cut-outs. Pupils will be involved by being invited to come and position selected items in the room plan.

Clearly there are many other instances involving build-ups, manipulation and addition of colour where the OHP is an effective instrument for the input of new language.

3   Language games

There are many games which are used to rework flashcards and to avoid new language recognition being repetitive and boring. All of these can be done on the OHP which also lends itself to many other games.

Memory games

1. *Which is missing?*

A variation on Kim's game, this can be played by hinging some cardboard flaps to the frame of a transparency containing new vocabulary illustrations (sports, foods, etc). After allowing the pupils to view the transparency, switch off, hinge over one or two flaps and ask the pupils to remember the missing items. This can be made simpler by suggesting alternative answers. A competitive element can be added to the game by having multiple flaps which reveal progressively more of the illustration and awarding fewer points as more of the illustration has to be revealed. 'Post it' labels of varying sizes are a speedier if less elegant alternative to this.

Kim's game itself can be played by cutting items out separately and laying them on the stage of the OHP, then switching the machine off and removing some of the objects.

2. *Which number?*

Overlay a transparency with numbers on top of a set of illustrations (e.g. school subjects, drinks, hobbies…), allow the pupils to memorise them, and then remove the overlay. Pupils can be asked to give either the number or the new word that matches the number. This could also be done with letters replacing the numbers, thus reinforcing the alphabet in the target language.

Memory games incorporating previous transparency suggestions

The acetate overlay containing town buildings (fig 5) could be removed and the pupils asked to remember where, for example, the cinema was. Using the target language, a group could be asked to direct the car to the cinema after which the overlay can be reinstated to check if they got it right.

Similar memory games could be played with overlays on a weather map (see page 6) or with prices on a fruit and vegetable stall.

A 'thief' could appear briefly on the OHP which is then switched off and the pupils asked to provide a description of the suspect including the clothes he was wearing. The transparency of the face (see fig 6) could also be used for this purpose.

Guessing games

1. *The keyhole game*

Cover the entire transparency with a piece of card in which has been cut a keyhole or any other interesting shape. Young pupils have great fun trying to suggest which object can be seen through the keyhole. Obviously you can have varying sizes of keyhole which reveal more or less of the picture beneath. This game can be played not only using individual illustrations but also using a scene which is gradually revealed. It is enjoyable **and** involves a considerable amount of language use as they try to work out how many people there are, where they are, what they are doing, what they are like... Two teams' suggestions can be recorded on the chalkboard, and final scores totted up for accuracy once the whole picture is revealed.

A variation of this game might be to reveal the scene for a few seconds only before the OHP is switched off and the teams asked to write, say or record what they remember.

2. *What is it?*

As another variation on the above, part of a silhouette shape or a transparency could be revealed and the pupils asked to suggest what they think it is.

3. *What is in the box/basket?*

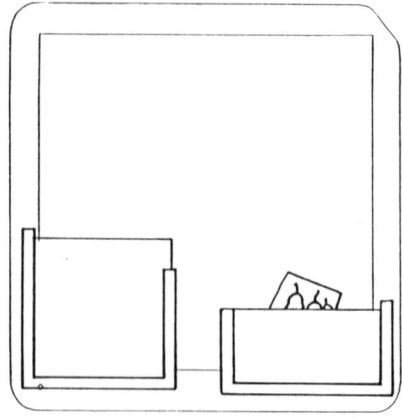

Prepare a transparency with large and small silhouetted boxes attached to it. Each week put in one shape or illustration relating to a new word or phrase met that week. End the week's classes by guessing what is in the boxes. This can motivate the pupils to learn new vocabulary, particularly if there is some incentive for guessing correctly (fig 8).

Card taped down to form two boxes into which cut out shapes can be slid.

Fig 8

4. What happened next?

Begin with one picture in a cartoon strip of nine and ask the pupils to suggest what happened next, gradually revealing the story line by adding overlays of each subsequent frame (fig 9).

Fig 9

... only a few of the 9 necessary overlays are shown. The others would be attached in a similar fashion.

5. What are they saying?

Prepare a transparency of two people speaking with empty 'speech bubbles'. A blank overlay would allow you to write in suggestions from the class (if you dare!), before adding an overlay with your suggestions in the bubbles (fig 10).

Fig 10 - from *Being Creative* by B Jones (CILT, 1992)

6. Call my bluff

A panel of four pupils sits with their backs to the OHP screen. A phrase, sentence or picture is shown on the screen and the rest of the class has to help the panel guess what is on the screen without using the actual words.

7. OXO games

The class is divided up in two teams - the X's and the O's. A grid of nine illustrations is produced as an overhead transparency and a blank sheet of acetate placed over it. The teams have to identify the items in the nine boxes. Each correct answer, in turn, results in adding an X or an O to the grid. The winning team is the first one with a line of three.

Note that the blank sheet over the grid means that the transparency can be used repeatedly without having to redraw the illustrations.

A modification of the game involves two teams sitting with their backs to the screen and two teams of 'supporters' (the class), in groups, take turns to help their teams guess one of the items on the screen to score an X or an O.

8. Pictionary

A pupil draws on the OHP using a phrase which only he or she can see. The target language can be used by the class to guess what is being drawn.

9. Matching

Labels cut in heavy acetate and bearing a word or phrase can be selected by pupils to place over the appropriate illustration on an overhead transparency. A little more reading is required in the following German example (fig 11).

Fig 11 - descriptions cut out of heavy acetate for selecting and placing on appropriate animal.

10. Spot the difference

Two similar pictures can be assembled side by side on the stage of the OHP and a blank overlay added. Differences spotted by the children can then be circled. Using a series of flaps which are gradually removed, a memory component can be added to the game (fig 12).

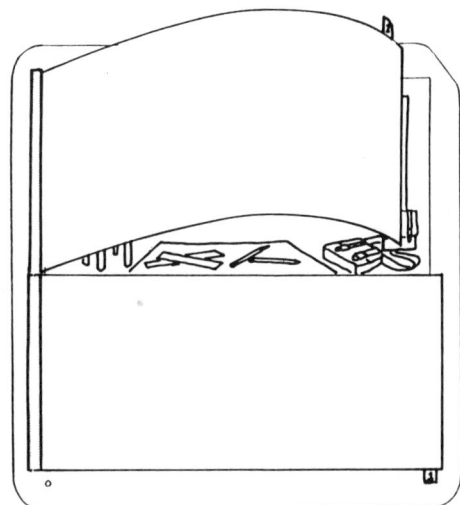

Fig 12

11. Blockbusters

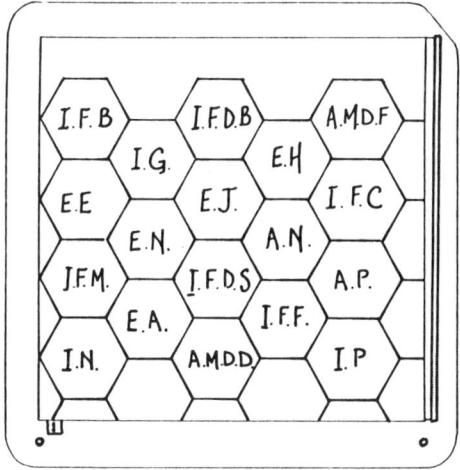

Prepare an overhead transparency of a blank grid (from e.g. Mary Glasgow's *Timesavers*) and prepare overlays which encourage pupils to guess the phrases and sentences on a particular topic e.g. the months, seasons and the weather in French (fig 13).

Fig 13   Motivators - e.g. E.E = *en été*.

13

4   Supporting the target language

We have already seen how the OHP can help the teacher to maintain the target language at the language input stage or in language games. However, we sometimes revert to English because we feel that a particular exercise is too complex to explain in the target language. One way of overcoming this is to demonstrate the exercise using the OHP.

Let's imagine that you wish to have pupils match phrases from, say, a white envelope, with pictures from a brown envelope. You could clearly show the class that you had two envelopes, take the pictures from one and lay them on the OHP and then the phrases from the other and do likewise. By **showing** the pupils and matching the pairs there would be no doubt as to what they were to do and no need to go into English to explain.

Grid completion

With some listening exercises pupils may not be clear about how to complete a grid. Grids can quickly be prepared for the OHP and the first example worked through with the class. Using overlays, other examples can be added later for correction of the exercise. As with most transparencies that you make, the time invested is well worth while when you consider how often you reuse the same resources.

Instructions for 'modelling'

Using the language for real purposes such as instructing how to make or do things can be well supported by means of the OHP. Simple recipes can be built up; the making of puppets by a teacher with a young class can be illustrated step by step by a series of overlays on the OHP. Complex activities can be explained before the 'real thing' is attempted. We well remember the visit of our Spanish exchange school during which we tried to explain the instructions for Scottish country dances in the gym. Prior stepwise (pardon the pun!) instruction on the OHP could perhaps have prevented a few bumps.

Class organisation

1. *Organising group work*

Groups can be informed of the various class activities in the target language provided there is visual support. This support can be most effectively supplied by overhead transparencies. A base transparency can show the room layout and the various activities. To this can be added an overlay showing what each group is to do and the order of work for the day (or week). A further overlay could indicate the names of the pupils in each group. Having a few extra overlays available would allow you to indicate the procedure for the changeover condition (fig 14).

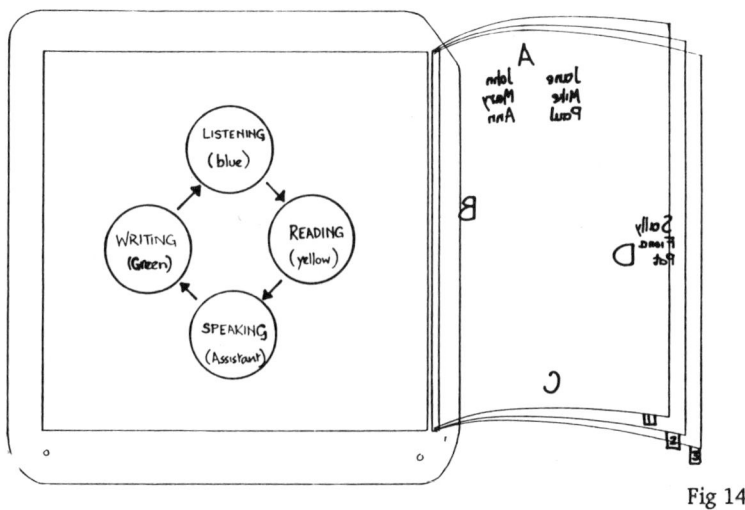

Fig 14

2. A menu system

The various activities on offer, e.g. telling the time, describing the seasons, or a specific unit, can be displayed on the OHP. Should you wish some pupils to have a more restricted choice, then their work could be highlighted by adding an overlay with specific names and programmes of work.

5   Teaching grammar

Overhead transparencies can easily be designed to help elicit a particular grammatical point, visually illustrate a particular concept, and to play language games designed to reinforce knowledge about the language.

Eliciting a grammatical point

Our own preference has always been to guide pupils towards the 'rule' after usage. Take, for example, the perfect tense in French. Pupils practise saying where they went on holiday, what they did, where they stayed, etc. As a final stage, they are asked these questions and the responses are inserted into the appropriate box on the overlay. This leads them towards the rules underpinning the previous usage.

Visual illustration

Graphic illustration of a concept may be more effective than long explanations. If we take the example of likes and dislikes in Spanish or Italian, pupils can be led towards grasping the concept if shown by visual means (fig 15).

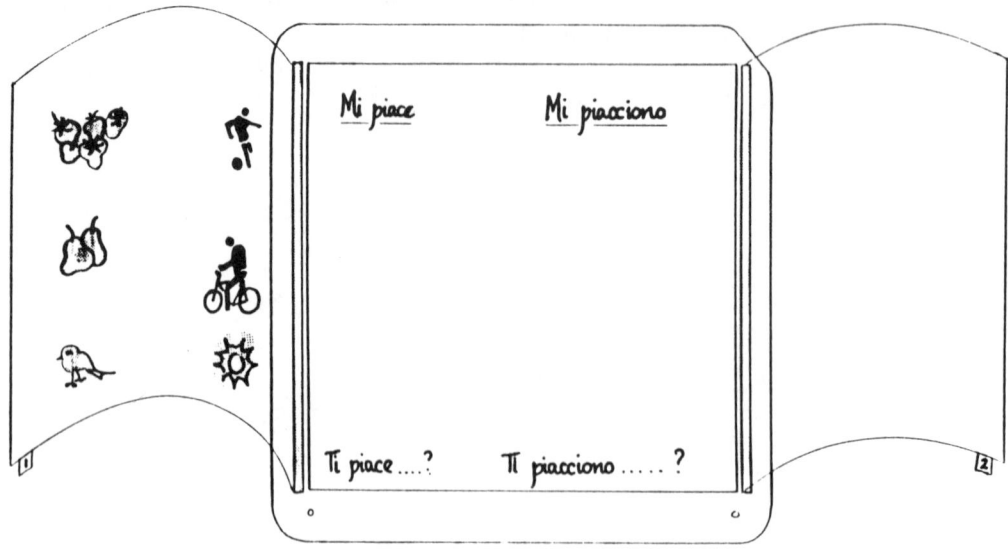

Fig 15

Base acetate   - telling what you like
                 - asking what they like

Overlay 1 - with visuals to aid 'grasping' the concept
Overlay 2 - blank - to write in your and their 'likes'

Grammar games

Beat the clock

Rearranging words on the OHP to form sentences can be a fun way of reinforcing grammatical points. Pupils choose a word from each of a variety of envelopes containing subject pronouns, auxiliary verbs, past participles, places and so on and are given a time limit in which they must form a correct sentence, if it is possible. If not, the next team adds its words until a successful sentence is achieved. Our colleagues teaching German assure us that this game is a good way of making 'word order' a little bit more interesting.

6 Songs and stories and surveys and things

There are so many more things that this most versatile resource can do. Here are just a few more.

Storytelling

Storytelling has played a successful part in the pilot language schemes in Scottish primary schools. Indeed, primary teachers have for years used their OHPs for storytelling. The story illustrations can be traced directly onto acetate, sometimes at size (if you're terribly lucky), sometimes after an initial 'enlarging' stage. The pupils themselves love to illustrate stories on acetate and there is a huge area of language to explore with their illustrations being projected and the text added as you go along in a series of overlays.

Songs

Sometimes the use of the OHP in a school is to project the words of the hymns for the weekly school assembly. This is valuable but a sterile way to use such a multipurpose tool. However, this particular technique is very valuable when we are teaching foreign language songs as the teacher can point to the words while the pupils are listening to the tape recording. Comprehension can further be assisted by the addition of graphics. For example, in the Spanish song 'Estaba la mora' there is frequent repetition and a new animal is added in each verse. A graphic of the animal would help comprehension, reinforce the new vocabulary and, with a bit of imagination, make the whole procedure a bit more entertaining.

Creating posters

At special festival times or to celebrate special events in your school, foreign language posters could be made for the classroom or corridor walls. An illustration is traced onto acetate and then projected onto a large sheet of poster paper on the wall. Pupils certainly enjoy this exercise. Just remember it's not art and though the end product will look much more professional than anything you or many of your pupils could ever achieve freehand, your art specialist colleagues will most probably disapprove. 'It stultifies your creativity' they say. Our usual reply to this is that if you don't have any creativity to stultify in the first place, it doesn't really matter!

Survey results

A popular communicative activity nowadays is the class survey. Presenting the collated results can be done most elegantly using the OHP. A variety of techniques for presenting data can be employed and will be discussed in more detail in the second part of the book .

Now this is where we stop. You will now, we hope, be fired with enthusiasm so read on: having dealt with the 'why', let's look at the 'how best to'.

7 Siting and using the OHP in the classroom

Just as the variety of uses of the OHP tends to be very restricted, so too does its effectiveness if it is badly positioned in the classroom. It is an overhead projector and yet you frequently see teachers standing with the OHP on a table and half the projected image obscured by the heads of both machine and the operator.

Positioning the projector

The projector should be placed on a low table or trolley so that:

★ the head assembly does not obstruct the view of the screen from any part of the classroom;

★ the work surface is at a convenient height for the teacher to write at while sitting down. This ensures that the teacher does not obstruct the view of the screen (fig 16).

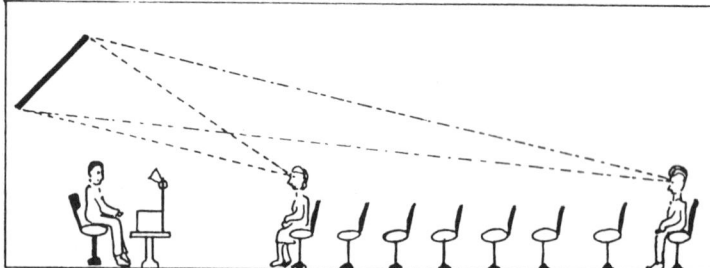

Ideally, the screen should be tilted forward to prevent 'keystoning' the image. Keystoning is the condition where a rectangular image, projected onto the screen, shows thus ⌴ . The technical term is 'trapezoidal distortion'.

Fig 16

The amount of tilt is decided by trial and error. Screen sizes vary. For most normal classrooms a 5' x 5' screen is best although in large lecture rooms as large as 10' x 10' may be required.

Using a 5' square screen, the projector will have to be about 7.5' away from it for the image to fill the screen using the standard lens which is normally supplied with the projector. This means that quite a large amount of floor space in a classroom is used up. This distance can be reduced if a special projector head is used. Normally this can be supplied with the projector in place of the standard head if it is requested when the OHP is purchased.

Position of the screen

Generally you find that classrooms are designed with a screen built in as part of the roller chalkboard or as a pull down structure which is situated above the board. If you have a choice, either because you are consulted at the design stage of your classroom (who would ever think of consulting a teacher?), or because you are working with a portable screen, then the most suitable position is shown below (fig 17).

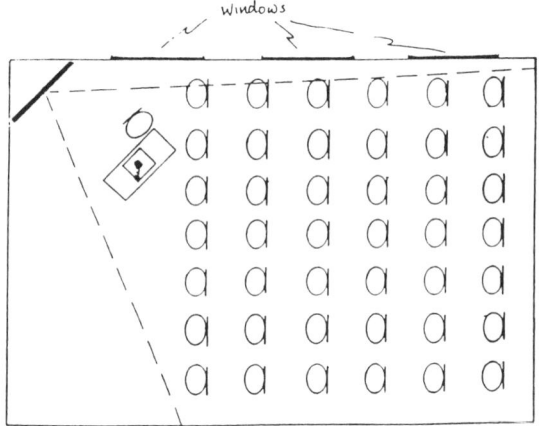

This presupposes that the classroom has windows against one wall. This corner arrangement minimises the amount of ambient light falling on the screen and allows the maximum number of viewers to be included within the accepted viewing angle (the dotted line in fig 17). This room layout also has the advantage that it clears a useful area of 'floor' space at the front of the room for setting up displays, demonstrations, and areas from which notes, other resources can be dispensed.

Fig 17

Positioning the teacher

Given this optimum room setting, the only thing left to arrange is yourself. It is always easy to spot the novice at using the OHP. You may look nervously over your shoulder at the screen, point with a long pointer at the screen or turn your back to the class and 'talk' to the screen at all times. None of this behaviour is necessary or desirable. You can, with the overhead projector, enjoy the luxury of facing the class **all the time**. Once the projector has been correctly aligned and focused (and you will have done this before the class comes in), details can be indicated on the transparency, using a pen (or even a finger), overlays can be added or removed, and written notes made **without looking at the screen**.

This set-up supports maximum communication between you and your class. You can see when there are gaps in comprehension occurring (the glazed look syndrome). You can see when there is the beginning of a discipline problem (Yes, we have had them too!) and you can divert the perpetrator before it becomes serious.

Finally, it is unlikely that every point in your lesson is being supported by transparency material, so be sure that you only have the machine switched on and the transparency projected **while it is relevant to the point you are making**. You will find that this technique directs the class's attention to **you** when you're speaking and back to the screen when you switch on again.

8   The 'raw materials'

Acetate

Most overhead projectors currently in schools have a platen providing a projected area of 10" x 10". Newer machines are appearing with a larger A4 platen (the long side of an A4 sheet, square). Acetate manufacturers make sheets of acetate to fit these standard sizes, usually in boxes of 50. There are different grades of acetate made (i.e. varying in thickness). Obviously, the thicker the acetate, the better the quality of the transparency and equally obviously, the thicker the acetate the more expensive it is. Generally speaking, the acetate sold in boxes come in three grades, 'light', 'medium' and 'heavy' weight.

There are some occasions when only the heavy weight acetate will do and we'll come back to this in the section on special effects.

For most of the things that you will wish to do the best compromise between cost and quality would be to go for the medium weight sheets. The light ones are not going to give you the kind of resource which will stand up to repeated use, to filing, to the addition and removal of overlays and to the general wear and tear of use as a departmental resource. (Oh, hadn't we mentioned that? Start making and using OHPT's effectively and you'll find you become the departmental resource specialist and provider!)

Seriously though, if you do put a lot of time and thought into producing good transparencies, you deserve to get many years use out of them. We mentioned in Section 1 that there were opportunities for the pupils to record their information, or illustrate their own stories on transparency. Clearly, here we could employ the light weight acetates since, with probably only a few exceptions, these would not be kept and used again and again.

Acetate is also supplied in 50' rolls and this can be mounted on the brackets which are provided with most projectors. These brackets can be moved so that the roll can move across the projector stage from side to side or from top to bottom.

Acetate which can be put through a photocopier or laser printer is also available. Please note that this is specially treated acetate and that normal 'write-on' acetate should never be put into any copier. It totally destroys the rollers at great expense, so unless you wish to be a candidate for early retirement, don't do it!

Card mounts (frames)

These are essential if

★   you plan to store and reuse transparencies

★   you are assembling transparencies with overlays attached.

Do not be convinced by the 'It must be able to fit into my A4 folder' group. This is making the resource fit your briefcase rather than your teaching objectives.

Card mounts are supplied, usually in boxes of 50, to fit the standard sizes of acetate sheet, by the suppliers of acetate.

Masking tape

This is the only tape which should be used for attaching acetates to mounts, hinging overlays and producing silhouette shapes on heavy acetate. Other adhesive tapes dry out after a few weeks, causing shrinkage and subsequent distortion of the frame. Masking tape also has the advantage of being the cheapest tape available.

Coloured adhesive film

When a large, even area of colour is required, the use of an OHP pen, no matter how broad the tip, is unsatisfactory. This problem is overcome by using coloured adhesive film. Various manufacturers produce such materials. It is better to choose ones which are described as 'low tack' or similar since these are easier to handle, can be lifted and repositioned and don't adhere to too violently until you rub them down. The best material which we have come across recently is produced by Stabilo and it's called Schwan Stabilo Self Adhesive Colour Film.

Dry transfer lettering

This material is similar in use to Letraset but is translucent and does not dry out or peel off when exposed to the heat of the projector lamp.

Project-a-type is one of the several types manufactured and is available in four colours and various letter sizes. It is costly but produces very professional results.

OHP pens

There are many manufacturers who produce pens specifically for writing on acetate. Please note that 'ordinary' fibre tip pens will not do. You find that if you attempt to use them they evaporate 'before your eyes' as soon as they come in contact with the heat of the projector lamp.

1. *Fibre tip OHP pens*

These come in two distinct categories:

★ **water based**. This type of pen contains ink which is water soluble. As a result, errors can be easily corrected when they occur by using a tissue or a cotton bud which has been slightly dampened - even 'lick' will do! Unfortunately, all water based liquids will also dissolve the ink, so coffee, spilled on the staff room table where you have laid down your precious OHPT, rain drops landing as you transport your acetate from one building to another, even the moisture of your fingers as you prepare the masterpiece - all will reduce your work to a multicoloured inky puddle. You may have deduced that we do not have a lot of time for water based pens!

★ **permanent or spirit based**. This type of pen contains ink which is soluble in alcohol. This means that the diagrams will not be easily accidentally damaged, unless someone spills a double vodka over them. In the case of errors, any fluid containing alcohol can be used to dampen the tissue or cotton bud. We have used methylated spirits, spirit duplicating fluid, in an emergency even perfume or brandy. (Few things present such a great emergency as that, we feel!)

Both types of pens dry out quickly if their caps are left off, but the spirit based type is extremely susceptible to this fault. However, if you train yourself always to replace the cap, even when you are laying the pen down for a few seconds to think, you will find that they last for months or even years without drying out.

The pens are available in a number of tip widths from extra fine to extra broad.

2. *Technical drawing pens*

Several manufacturers produce drawing pens which are intended for use in preparing office plans and maps. These are produced in a range of precise line widths. Some of these are extremely useful for OHP work, giving really sharp, very precise lines. The most useful ones for OHP work are 0.5mm for general lining, 0.7mm for lettering and 0.3mm for very fine lines. If extremely thick lines are called for, the 1mm point may be used. In all cases the ink used is drawing ink - usually black - and this can take a considerable time to dry but the quality of the end product is extremely high. For each of the above mentioned pens a stencil is available in a variety of type faces. This technique has to some extent been superseded by the arrival on the scene of desk top publishing.

Word processors and desk top publishing

This allows the producer of OHPTs to have access to a wide variety of type faces and sizes and indeed to drawing packages which result in really high quality images ready to be transferred, either by laserprinting or photocopying onto acetate.

The type of font you select is important. Don't be carried away by the very ornate. Simplicity should be the keynote with as large a point size as is necessary to meet the requirements of 'intelligibilty' as opposed to 'readability'.

24 point, bold in a sans serif typeface is about right. This one is Helvetica.

We are aiming at text which the pupils will read **and** comprehend when it is projected, whether or not they are giving it their full and undivided attention - that is 'intelligible'. Readable means that they **could** make out the words on the screen if they tried very hard and were not being distracted by other things.

As teachers it is **intelligibility** we are after!

9 Technical know-how

The OHP can be used to present facts and ideas in a number of ways. Its strength lies in its ability to build up the information step by step so that you, the teacher, can control the amount of information the class receives at a time, the rate at which additional information is added and the amount of revision/reinforcement that is needed.

Rolls v. sheets

1. *The acetate roll*

This is frequently used as a straightforward chalkboard replacement with the teacher writing directly onto it and winding it on to a fresh section of acetate roll as the existing one is filled up. This is not to be recommended for a variety of reasons:

(i)   It discourages forward planning - you just scribble down statements for your class to absorb but unlike the chalkboard you don't lose on discipline by turning your back on to the class to do so.

(ii) It encourages you to use your 'normal' handwriting which is too small to be read when projected.

(iii) It tempts you to indulge in the practice of having pupils copy down vast amounts of written material from the screen. Even in these days of belt tightening and cost efficiency this is not the best way to get information across - duplicated handouts are much more effective and you can then spend the time teaching the pupils rather than watching them writing!

If it is used as described above, as a continuous chalkboard, then as well as the educational undesirability of the technique, you find that the roll is soon filled up and has to be cleaned - a thankless task which will endear you to no-one when you request it. The repeated use of the roll in this way results in:

(i)   the acetates becoming scratched

(ii) the cleaned-off inks leaving a build up film of colour on the roll reducing the amount of light.

There are, of course, special occasions where the roll can be used most creatively and these will be discussed in the special effects section, later.

2. *Sheet acetates for producing mounted transparencies*

Using sheet acetate, material can be prepared for the OHP by either writing or drawing directly onto the acetate or by drafting out your plan first on paper and then transferring it by tracing or photocopying onto the acetate.

The acetate sheet is then taped to the back of a cardboard frame with masking tape round all four sides. It is false economy just to tape down the corners. Acetate is brittle and tears easily once a tiny cut is made on an edge, so that accidental damage from coarse handling on a desk or bundle of notes could mean an ugly tear across your precious work of art.

Presenting data

1. *Words on their own*

When you are presenting only words on your transparency, limit the number of words used. Edit your ideas to 'key' words and use them to lead your class towards the intended concept, with the OHP assisting you as you speak. Clearly there is a place for whole sentences, but not all the time. As a general rule: use a maximum of eight lines of text and limit each line to no more than eight words.

2. *Words with pictures*

Words with pictures should work together to reach the objective of the transparency. Generally speaking, titles are an unnecessary use of space on the transparency since the picture is only going to be on view while you are talking about it. Since your presentation is likely to go along the lines of *Voici la carte de la France avec les grandes villes...* you do not need to use some of your valuable drawing space with a beautifully lettered title. The title *La Carte de la France* is for your reference and will be on the card frame for ease of retrieval from storage.

3. *Words and numbers diagrams*

Words are, however, necessary for labelling, for axes on graphs, for scale units on graphs, for features on maps. But avoid using too many, particularly numbers. On graphs and charts, use only numbers to show the major divisions. Let the graph itself indicate the relationships and trends of the statistics.

On diagrams and charts it is important to decide where to put the words.

(i)   If a title is needed (remember, frequently it is not), place it at the top, but if there is a large empty space within the area of the diagram, you may choose, more informally, to include the title in that space.

(ii) Place all the labels so that they can be read without turning the acetate or the viewer's head. On graphs, the label for the horizontal axis should be directly below that axis. The label of the vertical axis should be place at the top of the axis parallel to the horizontal axis.

Lettering

There are several ways of producing successful lettering on OHPTs, and many unsuccessful ones. In the classroom, faced with constraints of which the major one will be finance, you will probably find that hand lettering is the only technique available to you. However, irrespective of the means of generating the lettering, there are some basic rules which must be followed.

1. *Style and spacing*

(i) Unless there is a very good reason for doing so (e.g. you are presenting some historical data and wish to create the right atmosphere with your OHPTs), choose a lettering style that is simple and does not use serifs - thin finishing strokes at the beginning and end of letters. This style is called sans serif, and is more suitable for projection since there are no thin strokes to be lost.

(ii) Use one lettering style throughout. If you do change the style, it must be for a specific reason, e.g. to emphasise important titles.

(iii) Use capitals (upper case) and small (lower case) letters. Lettering that is all in capitals is more difficult to read than text-style lettering which is a mix of upper and lower case. It is well documented that children who are slow readers find the reading of block capitals exceedingly difficult, and even those of us who do not have reading difficulties read faster and assimilate the information presented more rapidly if the print is not upper case.

(iv) Avoid *italicised* writing - if you wish to emphasise a phrase use colour, a slightly larger size or bolder lettering in the same style.

(v) Choose spacing that makes the words easier to read. A good rule of thumb is the 'n' notation. The letter 'n', in the same style as your lettering, is a good way to judge correct spacing.

Leave the space of one 'n' between words
two 'n's between sentences
three 'n's as a measure between lines
(baseline to baseline)

2. *Size*

Letter size should be at least 6mm for text. This is considerably bigger than most people's handwriting and the typeface on most standard typewriters. As mentioned before, 24 point font size is about right using a bold format on Applemac or similar.

When to use colour

1. To *differentiate*

Colour is useful for highlighting different elements within your transparency and leading the class to the kind of conclusions you want them to make. For example, the graph below shows the populations of four cities, A, B, C and D in the period from 1955 to 1990 (fig. 18).

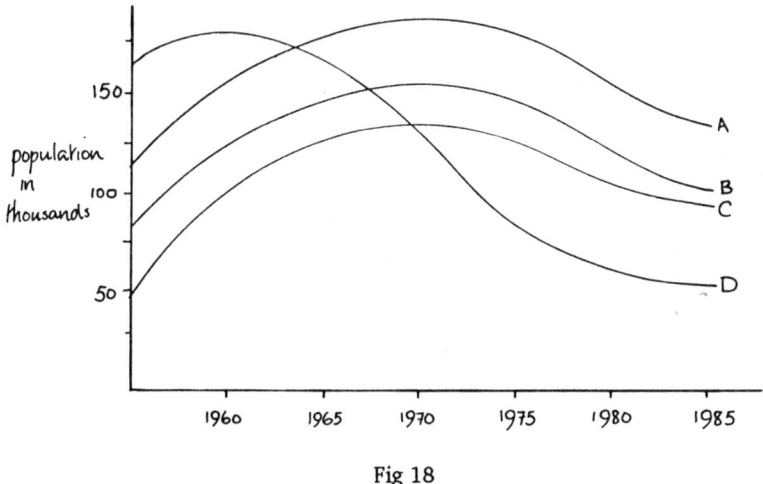

Fig 18

If each curve is drawn in a different colour it will lead pupils to make comparisons in trends between all the sets of data. They will compare what is happening in city A with city B, in city B with city C and so on. But if you make three of the curves, A, B, and C, the same colour and D a different colour, then you will be directing the class to look at the line that is different (i.e. D) and to compare it with the other three.

2. *To identify*

It is often useful to use some colour to indicate a certain type of information or section of a diagram over a series of transparencies since it helps the class to identify a particular element e.g. colour coding of the groups when organising group work will assist individuals to spot instantly to which group they are attached.

3. *To emphasise*

Colour is an excellent way to draw attention to a special element of your visual, but if you use too much colour emphasis is lost. If, for example, your OHPT has twenty words and you use five colours, nothing is special. If you only use two colours, there is sufficient contrast to make one of the colours show off special information.

4. *Sources of colour for overhead transparencies*

As we mentioned before in the section on raw materials, coloured pens are available in a maximum of eight colours including black. These are satisfactory for writing or drawing lines or for hatching (line shading).

If you require a solid area of colour, the pens will not do. If you colour in a solid area in this way it dries and gives a streaky effect when projected. The only way to achieve an acceptable result is to use a coloured adhesive film. Using the 'low tack' material described earlier, there are two methods of application possible:

(i) Trace out the shape required onto the back of the film, then cut it out with scissors or a blade. Then remove the backing and smooth the film down onto the acetate. Since it is difficult to write on the film, it is better to stick it onto the back of the acetate sheet and leave the face free for any writing. After you are certain the film is correctly positioned you can rub it down firmly thus ensuring a smooth layer which will not peel off. Be warned, get it right before you burnish it in this way because you will not shift it afterwards!

(ii) Cut a piece of coloured film slightly larger than the area to be covered. Apply it to the back surface peeling away the backing paper, bit by bit. When positioned, the excess can be carefully trimmed off using scalpel or other sharp blade. You must, of course, take care not to cut too deep or you also cut a hole in your acetate. Usually this technique should only be attempted if you are working with heavy weight acetate. When cut to size the film should be 'burnished' as before.

Occasionally, you may wish for a more flexible set of colours than the pens can provide. This would be the case if, for example, you were illustrating a story to tell children (there aren't many instances when faces can be coloured in using yellow, orange or red!).

In this case a stippling technique is appropriate. This involves laying down a series of dots of colours to be mixed and using a cotton bud dampened with solvent to 'paint' the colours together on the acetate. This technique takes a little practice but can achieve quite attractive results in both colour and texture.

We realise, of course, that there are ways of liberating masses of subtle colours onto acetate. All we need are computers with colour monitors, colour laser printers and the specially treated acetate sheets to feed through them. But until that great day comes, you'll get pretty good results using the methods we've mentioned above.

Special effects

There are several techniques which you can use which will maximise your overhead transparency, but remember that they will be effective only if they are suited to your objectives. Don't just use them for the sake of being different.

1. *Overlay*

This is probably the most useful technique which you will employ when using the OHP since it allows you to use the machine as a **teaching tool** - adding information **one step at a time** and presenting the information in a logical teaching sequence.

Overlays are additional transparencies which are used to build up (or break down) a visual idea, part by part. When designing the series of overlays to be used in a particular teaching sequence, it is worthwhile carefully setting down each of the teaching steps you wish to make since each one will be contained in a separate overlay sheet.

Each overlay - a whole sheet of acetate - is placed over the mounted base acetate and taped along one edge of the cardboard mounting frame. This means that each overlay can be 'flipped' on or off the base acetate as required.

Overlays can be mounted so that they can be used in any sequence with the base transparency (fig. 19). The overlays may have to be trimmed very slightly to make them fall easily into place. But care must be taken that the trimming does not result in the edge of the acetate showing up on the projected area.

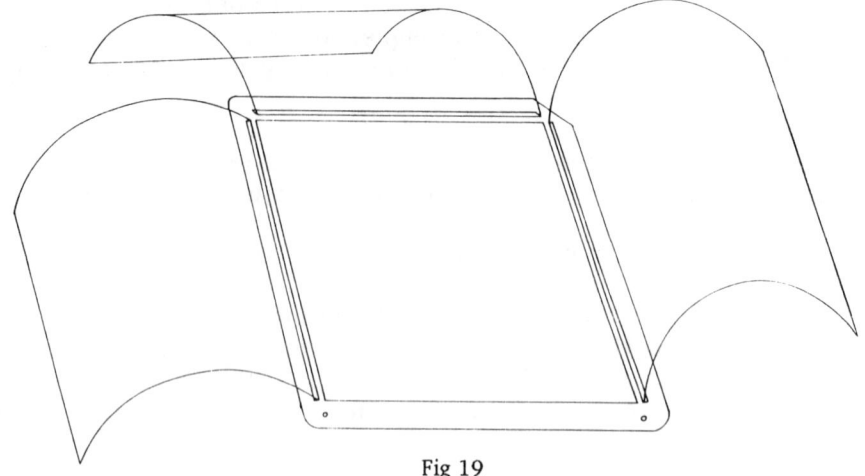

Fig 19

If the information in the overlays is always to be presented in the same fixed sequence, then the overlays can all be taped along the same side (fig. 20).

A useful addition is a little tab of masking tape which can be fixed to the edge of the overlay, making sure, of course, that it does not protrude into the projected area. If there are several overlays this greatly assists lifting them one at a time.

Fig 20

N.B. Never cut strips of acetate and tape them on as overlays. It is a false economy - neither doing the job as well nor looking anything like as professional.

Overlays can also be used in conjunction with an acetate roll which has been prepared in advance. The overlay is produced on an acetate sheet, mounted and placed on the stage of the OHP when the appropriate bit of the roll is being projected.

By preparing a mounted transparency which depicts the fixed part of a diagram or scene, movement can be introduced if the moving parts are drawn onto the roll of acetate which is then wound across the projector.

Telling a story with fixed characters encountering different situations as the action progresses could be dealt with in this way. Cast your mind back to the story of the little gingerbread man. (Go on, we're sure you remember it!) He encounters a horse, then a cow, then a sheep ... and so on until he meets the fox. All these characters could pass across the screen on the roll while the fixed acetate contains the principal character (fig. 21) - **or** the background landscape could be drawn on the acetate and all the characters added, when required, as cut outs (see p 34 on silhouettes).

Fig 21

Series of cut out shapes to support the adventures of the Little Gingerbread Man.

2. *Masking*

This is a quick and useful technique for presenting information on a transparency sequentially. It also provides the most economical use of acetate. It does, however, have the disadvantage that at the beginning of the presentation there is only a very small area of the screen lit and this does not look quite so impressive to the viewers as the whole area lit with items being added on whole overlay sheets. There are some instances though where it is quite acceptable.

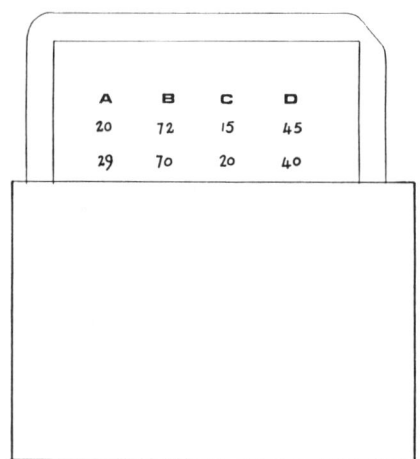

In its simplest form (and its least attractive!) a sheet of paper is placed over the transparency and can be pulled away to reveal information as required. Masks also provide the teacher with a visible 'cue sheet' since the unrevealed section of the transparency is visible to the teacher through the mask, while remaining invisible to the class (fig. 22).

Fig 22

More sophisticated forms of masking are achieved by preparing everything in advance, using the following procedure:

Cut a sheet of thin card into sections that fit those areas of the transparencies that you wish to reveal at one time. Hinge these sections onto the front of the card frame (again use masking tape for the hinges), aligning them so that they cover the appropriate sections of the transparency (figs. 23, 24). As you progress through your teaching sequence you can flip back the sections as and when you are ready to present that piece of information.

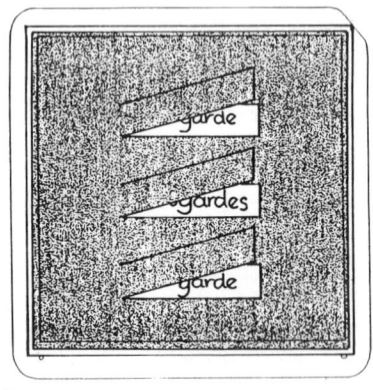

Fig 23

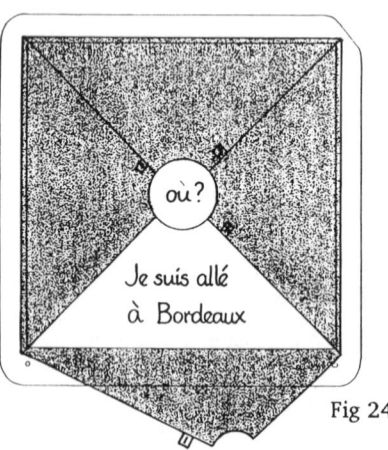

Fig 24

Clearly you can be more creative in your shape of masks depending on the nature of the material which you are presenting.

A further highlighting of the areas can be achieved by attaching coloured film to the back of the base acetate so that, as areas are revealed, they are highlighted in colour.

3. Using silhouettes

Since anything which is opaque will project as a black silhouette, we can use this technique to our advantage. In its simplest form a fine tipped pen or pencil laid on the screen will project as a pointer. So will your finger! You don't ever have to turn around and point directly at the screen.

Instead of your fingers, you could use cardboard arrows. They are simple to make and can be kept by the projector so that they can be added to any transparency to emphasise a point. All you need to make some arrows is some lightweight card, a pair of scissors and some glue (or double sided tape).

Cut a small arrow out of the card as shown below and a strip of card that is long enough to grip easily when folded into quarters, then assemble your arrows with their 'grips' which make them easier to move around on the transparency (fig. 25).

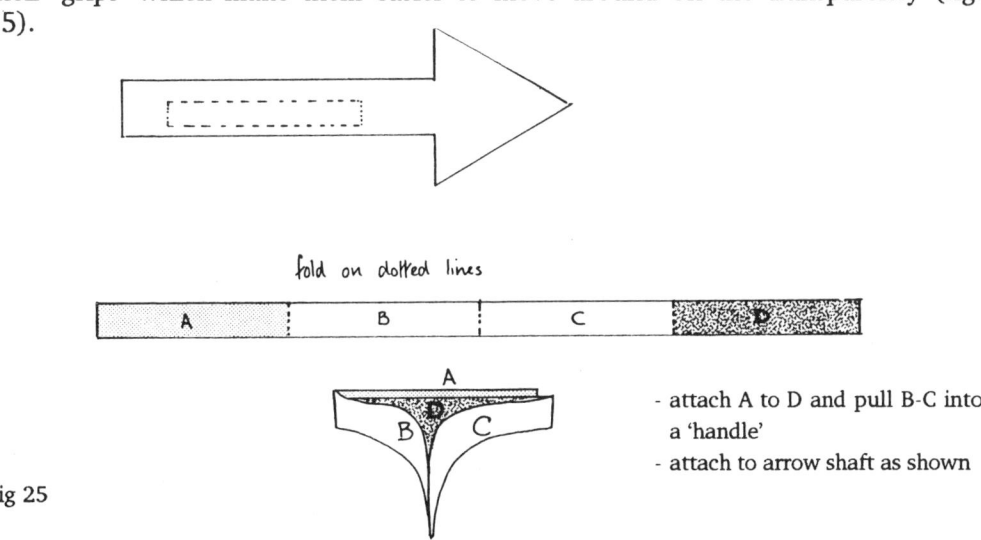

- attach A to D and pull B-C into a 'handle'
- attach to arrow shaft as shown

Fig 25

Silhouettes, as we have seen in chapter 2, can be used in a variety of ways, for animal shapes, for cut out figures to encourage story telling... this list could go on and on. Cut out of card and attached to strips of heavy acetate, they can be moved about the stage of the OHP and therefore can be manipulated to produce exciting shadow theatre scenes. This can be particularly effective when accompanied by dramatic music and could give rise to some very exciting language development.

Music that instantly springs to mind includes:

        Carnival of the animals   by Saint Saens
        Sorcerer's apprentice   by Dukas
        Peter and the wolf   by Prokofief

4. Using heavyweight acetate

If you are going to cut out shapes (illustrations or words) then you must use heavyweight quality of acetate. Anything else will fly away and be lost before your lesson has started. When you are cutting out words you are going to end up with lots of edges of acetate on show on the screen, so please keep dimensions uniform. Don't have some thin strips of acetate with lettering at one height, others thicker and at another height. The only variable should be the length of the word. And, please, use a straight edge and a sharp knife or scalpel to cut the acetate so that the projected edges are at least straight!

If you are cutting out a drawing of an object then you can disguise the cut edge by going over it with an OHP pen, after it has been cut out.

If you can persuade someone with access to thin clear perspex, to cut out a large number of centimetre squares for you, you have the wherewithall for a modern language OHP version of *Scrabble*. You can either hand write the letters on to each square or you can invest in a quantity of OHP dry transfer lettering.

5. Storytelling

If you're not feeling very creative, then your story illustrations can be traced from a book directly onto acetate sheets or a roll.

Otherwise, create your own illustrations or, often better still, have the class illustrate and tell the story themselves - the 10" x 10" format of acetates is an ideal size for pupils to draw on and even the most reluctant participant in class work is excited to see his work projected up the size of 5' square.

This is one of the occasions where stippling to obtain extra colours and effects is extremely useful.

10 In conclusion...

As you will probably have gathered, we are extremely enthusiastic users of this very user friendly, fairly inexpensive and universally available technology. We hope that we have convinced you that it can improve your presentation skills as it has ours. Whatever the sophistication or lack of it that a transparency demonstrate, however, it should fulfil the teaching objectives for which it was created and this means planning.

Good OHPTs don't just happen - they are designed. And they are designed, not by graphic artists, not by computer whiz kids but by good teachers. They are the people who know what has to be presented and they are the only ones who know the steps of that presentation. So don't be frightened into thinking that someone else should be making these. They are well within your capabilities - all you have to do is get started.

Remember, design the end product on paper first, then trace off the bits, one step at a time, on to acetate, and you'll have a resource which you'll use for many years to come.

So, off you go and have fun!

Appendix: Maintenance and care

Although you may feel that this is not within the remit of the language teacher, it is worthwhile noting that OHPs in schools frequently don't work as well as they should and people complain that the picture isn't very bright. This is particularly true where there is also a chalkboard in the room. A sensational improvement can be effected by weekly cleaning!

1. ... of the machine

The fan

All OHPs have a cooling fan to keep the lamp and machine from overheating. Two types of switching are commonly used:

(i) The fan is switched on when the machine is switched on but is thermostatically controlled and will not switch off again until the machine has cooled down.

(ii) The fan is switched on and off independently of the lamp.

Whichever system is used, the fan must never be switched off at the same time as the lamp but must be allowed to stay on for about five minutes longer than the lamp.

Movement

The projector should not be bumped or moved while the lamp is hot since this greatly reduces the length of life of the lamp.

Dim/bright switch

Some machines have a switch which enables them to run with the lamp about 10% under the full brightness. In most situations this difference is barely noticeable, but it does increase the life of the lamp by a factor of two to three. This is an extremely worthwhile economy and should be used whenever possible.

Cleaning

The overhead projector collects dust rapidly and it is well worth cleaning the machine regularly since the accumulation of dust can cut down light transmission.

The following parts should be cleaned with warm water, containing a drop or two of washing up liquid, and a soft cloth (fig. 26).

Surfaces requiring regular cleaning.

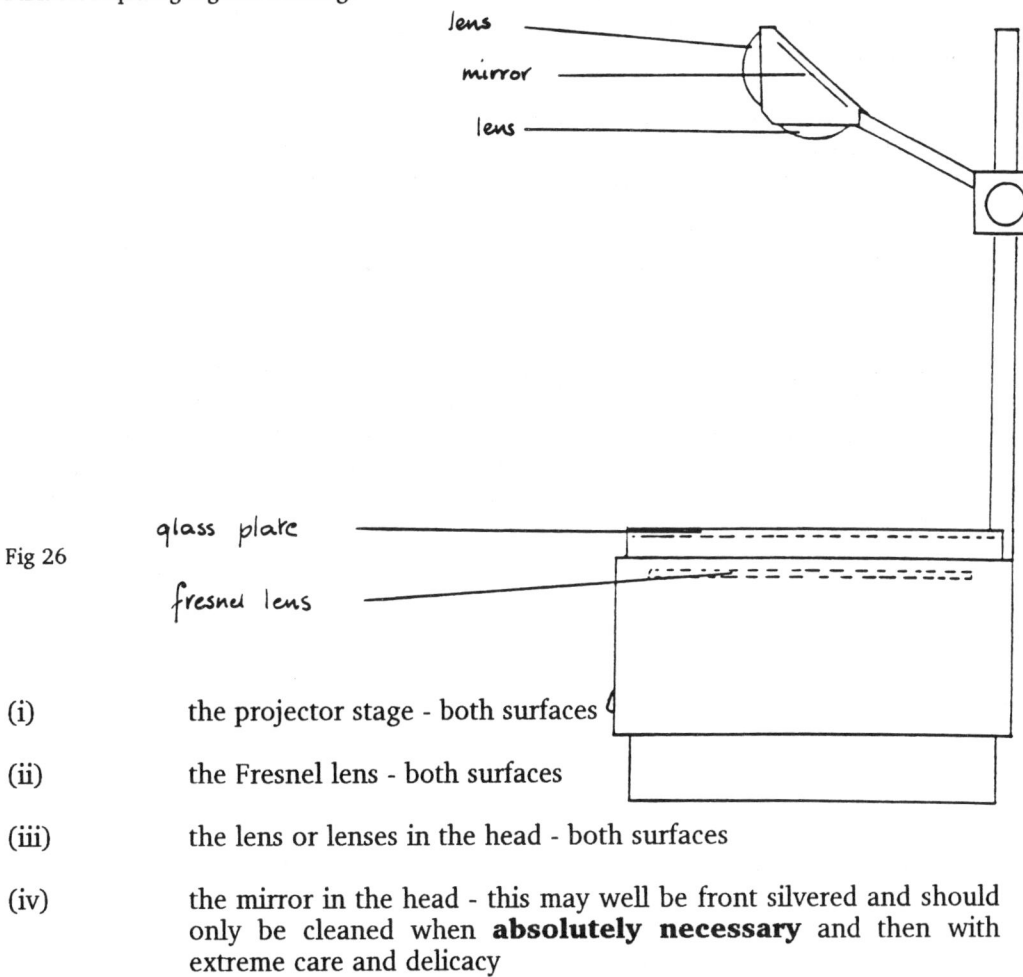

Fig 26

(i) the projector stage - both surfaces

(ii) the Fresnel lens - both surfaces

(iii) the lens or lenses in the head - both surfaces

(iv) the mirror in the head - this may well be front silvered and should only be cleaned when **absolutely necessary** and then with extreme care and delicacy

All these parts should be dried immediately after cleaning.

2. ... *of the acetates*

Once you have become 'hooked' on the production and use of overhead transparencies, you are faced with the problem of storage and retrieval. You will have rapidly discovered that normal sized brief cases are too small to hold OHPTs mounted on their frames, and carrying them about in a polybag is scarcely conducive to maintaining them in good condition (and it doesn't do much for your image either!). The solutions are not ideal and tend, like most other areas we have dealt with, to be dictated by cost.

1. Manufacturers do supply storage/filing boxes for OHPTs. They usually store the units vertically and allow for ease of finding individual transparencies within the box.

2. We have adopted the DIY storage box system where we have a local box manufacturer make up brown cardboard boxes of the right size - much cheaper than 1 above but we have to buy 100 at a time.

3. If you are old enough, and spent your salad days collecting 12" LP's you'll probably have carrying cases for these records. The 10" x 10" frames fit these boxes perfectly.

4. For the young (who in their youths 'built things' out of cardboard) you can always make a carrying case with two bits of heavy card (mounting board or the sides of packing boxes that household appliances come in are ideal) folded into a primitive 'folio' and hinged with parcel tape. If you are feeling creative, you can add handles and any other personal touch that comes to mind.